About the Author

When Naomi is not photographing mushrooms in the wilds of Victoria or staring at the clouds, she works as a narrative game writer, theatre director, poet and a joyful children's book collector.

About the Illustrator

All Sunshine wants to do is spread a bit more hope and creativity to people's lives! She exhibits an infectious positive energy through her illustrations, and on Twitch and YouTube. Sunshine illustrates her joyful characters using a blend of traditional mediums in a variety of illustration styles.

For Ailith Rose, whose kite flying makes me feel lighter than air. NW

First published by Ford Street Publishing, Melbourne, Victoria, Australia

2 4 6 8 10 9 7 5 3 1

Title: *Wendy, Weather Watcher: Blown Away*

ISBN 9781922696526

First published 2025

A catalogue record for this book is available from the National Library of Australia

Printed in China by Tingleman Pty Ltd

Wendy, Weather Watcher

By Naomi Woodward

Illustrations by Sunshine

CHAPTER ONE:

Windy Weather

Wendy loved a windy day.

The kind of windy day when her rainbow umbrella popped inside out.

The sort of windy day when she watched the pinwheel in the garden *spin* until she felt dizzy.

The type of windy day when paper boats rushed along the gutters and clouds *swirled* in interesting shapes across the sky.

You see, Wendy was a 'Weather Watcher'.

Wendy's mum and dad were meteorologists. Each day they went to work and studied weather from all over the world.

They made very important notes on what they found for important people, including the nice weather reporter on the news.

Wendy's parents said that even though she was still a kid, she could look outside and make her own notes about the weather too, and THAT made Wendy a Weather Watcher!

Wendy woke up to a rustling outside her bedroom window.

Jumping out of bed to look, she watched a pile of leaves blow across the ground, from one side of the garden to the other.

Wendy's pet parrot, Radar, flapped excitedly around the bedroom.

'Windy day! Squawk! Windy day!'

'I have a hunch that today is a good day for kite flying.' Wendy smiled at Radar. 'But first, we need to check a few things, just to be sure that it really is a *windy* day!'

Wendy and Radar searched around the garden for windy weather clues to put in her notebook.

'We can't see the wind,' said Wendy, 'but we can feel the wind and see what it can do!'

The leaves that her dad had raked into a neat pile now danced merrily around her feet. Beside the flower bed, Wendy lay flat on her stomach and inspected a patch of grass. A ladybird was busy balancing on a grass blade that was bending to and fro. Even the towels on the washing line waved about, drying in the breeze.

Radar flew up into the branches of a tree, where he could hear its leaves *swishing*.

'Mum taught me an *easy* way to find out which direction the wind is blowing from,' said Wendy. She stood very still, wet her pointer finger with her tongue and held it up to the sky. Radar tilted his head. How

15
100

could Wendy's finger tell which way the wind was blowing?

'My finger is facing the garden fence. Dad says that's North. And when I hold up my wet finger, the ball of my finger feels extra cold from the wind!' Wendy thought hard. 'The wind is blowing from the north!' she shouted, then wrote it down in her notebook.

Impressed, Radar flapped his wings.

Next, Wendy and Radar checked her parents' anemometer, a special machine that measures the speed of the wind. The cups on the anemometer moved steadily round in a circle, getting faster and faster as the wind grew stronger.

Wendy's dad stood at the back door, surveying the weather. 'Be careful,' he joked. 'Radar might be blown to the research station all the way in Antarctica!'

Wendy grinned at Radar. 'That's more than enough wind to lift a kite into the sky! Today is the PERFECT day for flying a kite!'

CHAPTER TWO:
Building a Kite

Wendy looked for the materials she needed to build her very own kite. She was always making fun things out of odd bits she found around the house, and she knew exactly where to start!

'Craft drawer! Squawk! Craft drawer!' Radar squawked.

Wendy picked out a sheet of shiny red paper, a roll of sticky tape and a pair of scissors from her craft drawer.

She found her parents at the kitchen table. Spread out in front of them was a big map of the town and the surrounding farmlands. They were both busy drawing lots of squiggly lines on the map in pencil.

'Paper kite! Squawk! Paper kite!' Radar landed on the middle of the map.

Her mum gently brushed Radar aside. 'Have you looked in the birthday bag under the stairs?' she asked.

'You might find something useful in my barbecue box,' said her dad as he drew an extra long squiggle across the map.

In the cupboard under the stairs, Wendy rummaged through a bag full of party poppers, wrapping paper and blank cards until she found yellow streamers and a ball of brightly-coloured string left over from her birthday party.

Then she took two long skewers from her dad's barbecue box.

With her arms full, Wendy carried the items to her bedroom. Radar flew close behind, dangling the ball of coloured string from his feet.

Wendy laid out all the materials on her bedroom floor.

She carefully folded and cut the shiny red paper. Then she laid the two long skewers like a cross on the paper and taped them in place.

Finally, she poked a hole at the bottom of the paper and threaded the coloured string through.

'Yellow bows! Squawk! Yellow bows!'

'Yellow bows are EXACTLY what this kite needs!'

Wendy was tying the final bow on her kite when her mum walked in. She was holding Wendy's favourite green scarf and matching gloves.

‘There’s no time for kite flying, Wendy,’ her mum said. ‘Your Aunt Amelia has a special windy surprise for you!’

A windy surprise? wondered Wendy. What could it possibly be?

CHAPTER THREE:
Up, Up and Away!

Wendy loved her Aunt Amelia even more than she loved windy days!

She was an explorer.

Aunt Amelia ALWAYS had an exciting surprise.

On a hill not far from Wendy's house, her aunt was waiting for them. She was dressed in silk parachute pants and an old aviator jacket.

Wendy and Radar couldn't believe their eyes.

Aunt Amelia's windy surprise was a HOT AIR BALLOON!

She beamed at Wendy. 'Have you seen a party balloon being carried by the wind? Well, a hot air balloon is BIGGER and BETTER!'

The hot air balloon was taller than

Wendy's house. It had four stripes in different colours – purple, yellow, pink and blue. Below the balloon, a brown wicker basket was attached to it with strong ropes.

'Good thing you're wearing your scarf and gloves. It can be pretty cold way up high in the air,' said Aunt Amelia. 'Is Radar coming too?'

Radar flew up and circled the balloon with a cheeky flap of his wings.

'I think Radar is going to use his own wings to fly instead!' Wendy laughed. 'He is a bird after all!'

'Radar's wings! Squawk! Radar's wings!'

Wendy climbed into the basket and looked around curiously. The basket was empty.

'Where's the steering wheel?' she asked.

'There isn't one!' said Aunt Amelia. 'The wind lifts the balloon and carries it. The direction we go in depends on which way the wind is blowing at different altitudes.'

'Like a bubble!' exclaimed Wendy.

In the centre of the balloon was a lever attached to a burner. Each time Wendy pulled the lever, a burst of flame heated up the air inside the balloon, making the balloon rise higher and higher and higher!

Up . . . Up . . . UP the hot air balloon went until it was floating serenely through the sky.

Except for the short burst of flame every now and then, the hot air balloon hardly made a sound.

Wendy grinned as they dreamily travelled along. 'It's quieter than an aeroplane,' she said.

From her view in the basket, Wendy could see the tops of houses and trees, and the people in the town below scurried about like ants.

'These will make exciting pictures,' said Wendy, thinking of how she would sketch it all in her notebook later.

She could even touch the clouds. She waved to Radar, who was gliding on the wind beside them.

'Sheep and Cows! Squawk! Sheep and Cows!'

'Uh-oh!' Aunt Amelia's eyebrows knitted together. 'Radar is right. That's farmland below us. The wind has changed direction and is carrying us off-course, away from the town.'

Oh no! thought Wendy, her stomach twisting into a knot. She had never been this far from her home before. Soon they would be lost, floating somewhere in the sky! What were they going to do?

CHAPTER FOUR:

Blown Away

The hot air balloon was floating further and further away from the town. Aunt Amelia studied her map.

'We're so high up, all the hills look the same to me!' she said, frowning. 'I guess hot air balloons are not always the most reliable way to travel! We'd better find someplace safe to land.'

Wendy peered at the ground far below. How were they ever going to land their giant balloon?

'Getting down is easy enough,' said Aunt Amelia. 'We need to find somewhere to land that is away from animals and crops. I don't think a farmer would be too happy with us landing on top of his wheat field.'

Wendy searched the ground for an

empty field. But everywhere she looked, she saw nothing but paddocks with cows and farmhouses with ponds.

'We can't land here!' groaned Aunt Amelia. 'We'll end up right in the middle of that pond. I don't feel like swimming today!'

'Over the hill! Squawk! Over the hill!'

'It's Radar!' shouted Wendy. 'He knows where we can land the hot air balloon!'

With a final burst of flame, the balloon floated up. Wendy held her breath as they followed Radar and drifted over a hill. What would they find on the other side?

Bit by bit, a wide green stretch of land appeared on the other side of the hill.

'It's as flat as a pancake!' whooped Aunt Amelia.

'And not a farm in sight!' cried Wendy. 'Is this a safe place to land the balloon?'

'Sure is!' cheered Aunt Amelia. 'Brace yourself, Wendy. Bend your knees and hold on to the ropes. Our ride is about to get bumpy!'

CHAPTER FIVE:

Breezy Landing

DOWN . . . Down . . . Down went the hot air balloon!

Aunt Amelia pulled open a large vent at the top of the balloon. Whoosh! The hot air was released from the balloon, making it heavier.

The ground below grew closer and closer and CLOSER! Wendy crouched lower in the basket to brace herself.

'HOLD ON TIGHT!' shouted Aunt Amelia. 'Here comes the BUMP!'

Wendy held on to the basket as tightly as she could. She squeezed her eyes closed and . . .

BUMP!

BUMP!

BUMP!

When Wendy opened her eyes, the balloon was safely on the ground.

'See!' said Aunt Amelia. 'Landing is a breeze! And we found the perfect spot to set down, thanks to Radar! Three cheers for Radar! HOORAY!'

'Breezy landing! Squawk! Breezy landing!'

Climbing out of the basket, Wendy looked around their landing spot. The beautiful balloon was now lying deflated on the ground.

'But how are we going to get home?' asked Wendy.

‘I think your mum and dad have the answer,’ said Aunt Amelia, pointing towards a nearby road. ‘Look who’s coming!’

Sure enough, Wendy’s parents were racing down the road with a trailer hooked to the back of their car. They soon pulled up beside the deflated balloon.

‘How did you know where the hot air balloon would land?’ Wendy asked them.

‘It’s our job to know about windy weather,’ said her dad. ‘That’s what our weather map is for.’

‘Our scribbly lines mark the directions and speed the wind is blowing today,’ said her mum. ‘We’ve been storm chasers before, but this is our first time being balloon chasers!’

‘It’s easy to get *carried away* with hot air ballooning!’ Her dad winked. ‘Next time your aunt goes hot air ballooning, we’ll make sure she has a *weather* map.’

Wendy smiled as Radar settled on her shoulder. 'Hot air balloons are an exciting way to travel,' she said. 'But I think I'll keep my two feet on the ground for a while!'

Back home in the garden, Wendy held tightly to one end of brightly-coloured string. High in the sky, her shiny red kite darted about, the yellow bows waving in the breeze.

Today was the PERFECT day for flying a kite!

Wendy's Weather Watcher Words

Altitude: The height of something above sea level.

Anemometer: A device used to measure the speed and the force of wind.

Burner: The engine of the hot air balloon that produces flame and heat.

Meteorologist: A scientist who studies what makes particular weather conditions.

Weather Map: A map using symbols and lines to show what the weather will be at a certain place in time.